LEONTYNE PRICE

Singing Star

Kristen Woronoff

BLACKBIRCH PRESS

Detroit • New York • San Diego • San Francisco
Boston • New Haven, Conn. • Waterville, Maine
London • Munich

Published by Blackbirch Press
10911 Technology Place
San Diego, CA 92127
e-mail: customerservice@galegroup.com
Web site: http://www.galegroup.com/blackbirch

© 2002 Blackbirch Press
an imprint of the Gale Group

All rights reserved. No part of this book may be reproduced in any form without permission in writing from Blackbirch Press, except by a reviewer.

Printed in China

10 9 8 7 6 5 4 3 2 1

Photo credits:
Cover, cover inset, pages 21, 23, 24 © Metropolitan Opera Archives; pages 3, 9, 13, 15, 17, 20, 22, 25, 26, 30 © Schomburg Center for Research in Black Culture/New York Public Library; pages 4-5 © The Library of Congress; pages 6, 10 © National Archives; page 12 © Henry Grossman/courtesy of Communications Office, The Juilliard School; pages 21, 56, 59 © AP/Wide World Photos

Library of Congress Cataloging-in-Publication Data
Woronoff, Kristen.
Leontyne Price / by Kristen Woronoff
   p. cm. — (Famous women juniors)
Includes index.
Summary: A biography of the African-American woman who overcame racism and segregation to become one of the greatest opera singers of the twentieth century.
        ISBN 1-56711-589-6 (hardcover : alk. paper)
1. Price, Leontyne—Juvenile literature. 2. Sopranos (Singers)—United States—Biography—Juvenile literature. [1. Price, Leontyne. 2. Singers. 3. African Americans—Biography. 4. Women—Biography.] I. Title. II. Series.
ML3930.P745 W67 2002
782.1'092—dc21   2001005132

For more than twenty-five years, Leontyne Price was one of the most famous opera singers in the world. She was also the first African American superstar in the world of opera. Her hard work, courage, and great musical gifts have made her a role model to Americans everywhere.

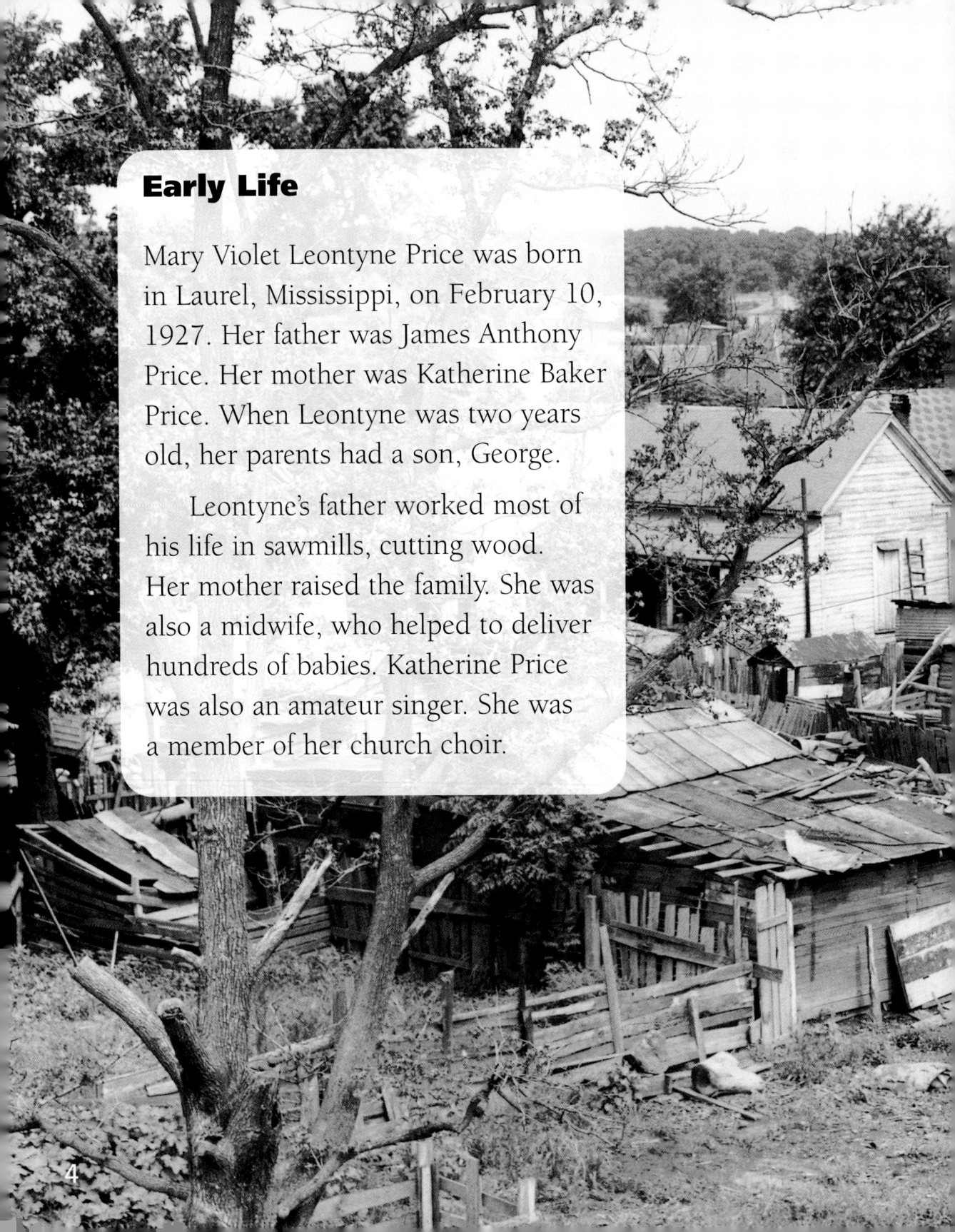

Early Life

Mary Violet Leontyne Price was born in Laurel, Mississippi, on February 10, 1927. Her father was James Anthony Price. Her mother was Katherine Baker Price. When Leontyne was two years old, her parents had a son, George.

Leontyne's father worked most of his life in sawmills, cutting wood. Her mother raised the family. She was also a midwife, who helped to deliver hundreds of babies. Katherine Price was also an amateur singer. She was a member of her church choir.

Leontyne was born in Laurel, Mississippi.

Leontyne grew up with music all around her. Her parents knew that their daughter had a gift for music from a young age. When she was four years old, Leontyne started taking piano lessons. Even though she was an excellent piano student, it was her singing voice that everyone noticed.

When Leontyne was a child, the South was segregated. That meant many places were closed to African Americans.

During Leontyne's childhood, the South was a place where people were judged by their skin color. Most of the South was segregated, or divided by race. African Americans lived on one side of town. Whites lived on the other. The Price family lived in the African American neighborhood in Laurel. Throughout the South, African Americans and whites went to different churches and schools. They ate in different restaurants and stayed in different hotels.

Around Laurel, many African American men worked in the lumber industry. Some African Americans—both men and women—worked as servants in the homes of wealthy white people. Leontyne's aunt, Everlina Greer, was a maid for a white man named Alexander Chisholm.

As young children, Leontyne and her brother often went with their Aunt Everlina when she went to work. The Chisholms had children who were almost the same ages as Leontyne and George. The Price children and the Chisholm children became friends, and so did their parents.

The Chisholms soon heard young Leontyne singing. They asked the young girl to sing at parties they gave. As Leontyne entered her teenage years, other people around Laurel also heard the amazing sound of her singing. Her voice rang out at her high school, Oak Park Vocational High School. She also sang at most major musical events in town, from weddings to parties.

Leontyne began singing at a young age. By the time she was in high school, she was recognized as a special talent.

An American soldier stands guard at Iwo Jima during World War II.

To College and a Career

In 1944, when she was 17, Leontyne won a scholarship to Central State University in Ohio. At that time, the United States was at war with Germany and Japan. The military, like most of the country, was segregated. Soon, her brother George entered the army and learned about that prejudice. Yet he rose to the rank of general. Like her brother, Leontyne was determined to rise above the small-minded people who judged others by skin color.

Leontyne studied music at Central State University in Ohio.

At Central State, Leontyne studied to become a music teacher. Soon, however, her classmates and teachers heard her sing. They told Leontyne that she should study to become a singer. She followed their advice and changed her major to voice.

After several years at Central State, Leontyne decided she wanted to attend the Juilliard School in New York City. Juilliard is one of the most widely known music schools in the world.

But the cost of going to Juilliard was very high. Luckily, Leontyne's classmates and teachers gave a special concert to help her raise money. The Chisholm family, who had known about Leontyne's talent for years, also gave money to help her continue her education.

Moving to New York City was a big change for Leontyne. It was a big, busy city, unlike any place she had ever lived. The biggest change, however, was in the music she studied. Until that point, she had sung only popular songs or religious music. She knew very little about opera music. Opera is a play set to music, with words sung or spoken while an orchestra plays. New York City was the center of opera in the United States. In the city, Leontyne attended the opera. When she heard opera at the Metropolitan Opera, she suddenly knew what her goal was. She wanted to become an opera singer.

At Juilliard, Leontyne's voice teacher, Florence Kimball, knew right away that her new student had unusual talent. She helped Leontyne learn the soprano, or higher, notes. Florence believed that with the right training, Leontyne could sing almost anything in opera written for a soprano. Italian composers wrote the most famous operas with soprano parts.

While attending Juilliard, Leontyne decided to become an opera singer.

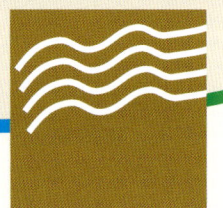

One of Leontyne's first opera roles was in a student performance at the Juilliard School. She sang in *Falstaff*, an opera by the famous Italian composer Verdi. A music critic from a large newspaper saw the performance and could tell Leontyne was talented. He knew she would be a star.

News of the Juilliard student with the powerful voice spread around the New York music business. This led to Leontyne's first job offer. It was not a role in which she would sing classical Italian opera. Instead, she was asked to take a part in a production of *Porgy and Bess*, an American opera written in the 1930s.

Leontyne and William Warfield (right) rehearse for *Porgy and Bess*.

The producers of *Porgy and Bess* had heard about Leontyne. They had been at a performance of *Falstaff*. They had brought with them the famous singer, William Warfield, who was also cast for *Porgy and Bess*. After the show, they went backstage. Leontyne and William met for the first time that night.

Porgy and Bess started its U.S. tour in Dallas, Texas in 1952. Leontyne began to understand what it would be like to be famous. Her performance was a hit. But despite the good reviews for the show, discrimination was still common in the South. The cast was all black. They had trouble making hotel reservations and getting served in restaurants.

After Dallas, the tour stopped in Chicago, Illinois. William decided he would ask Leontyne to marry him. At dinner one night, he planned to put an engagement ring on Leontyne's finger while her hands were underneath the table. By accident, he dropped the ring. He had to crawl beneath the table to find it. When he finally found it, he proposed. The two married on August 31, 1952. Soon after that, the tour of *Porgy and Bess* went on to Europe.

Leontyne married William Warfield in 1952.

Leontyne began performing on television. Millions of people from all over the country were now able to see how talented she was. Through television, Leontyne found success and stardom. Her first television appearance was in the opera *Tosca*, by Giacomo Puccini. She played an Italian woman. Her performance was a hit.

Leontyne sang in the opera *Tosca*, which was shown on national television.

Leontyne took more television roles. She also performed in opera houses in the United States and Europe. Finally, Leontyne made her debut at the Metropolitan Opera in New York City. She sang the role of *Aïda*, a slave-princess. That is the role she is most identified with.

Leontyne practiced for the part every day. She sang notes and did voice exercises.

Leontyne performing as Aïda.

She devoted almost all of her time to learning and practicing new roles. Her life consisted of three things—practicing, resting, and eating.

Leontyne and William spent whatever time they had together at their house in New York City. But they both knew they had changed a lot since they had gotten married. Leontyne was a young girl when they first met. Now she was famous. She was too busy to spend a lot of time with her husband.

Leontyne and William realized they were on different paths. In 1958, they separated. Their divorce did not come until 1972, but they have always remained close friends.

Leontyne and William separated in 1958.

Leontyne performed at the Metropolitan Opera (the "Met") for the first time on January 27, 1961. She was 33 years old. Her parents, her brother, and the Chisholms were all in the audience. When she finished, the audience stood and cheered for more than 45 minutes.

Leontyne performed at the Met throughout her career. She performed some of her most famous roles there. One of the most important events for a singer is to perform on an opening night at the Met. Leontyne was asked to open the 1961–1962 season. She was the first African American ever to do it.

Even though she was one of the world's most successful opera singers, Leontyne always pushed herself to do more.

Later in 1961, Leontyne was working too hard. She had many performances, and she lost her voice at one point. Her doctor told her she had to take a break from singing. Her illness taught her that she needed to be more careful.

In 1966, Leontyne received another great honor. It was the last year the Metropolitan Opera would perform in the old opera house on 39th Street. In September, the opera moved to a new building at Lincoln Center. A goodbye party was held, and Leontyne was asked to sing that night.

The Metropolitan Opera performed in this building until 1966.

After her performance, Leontyne took part in an unusual ceremony. The old curtain at the Met stage was not going to be moved to the new location. It was going to be cut up into 45,000 small pieces. These pieces would be included in a record album. At the ceremony, Leontyne took a pair of scissors and cut the first piece of the old curtain.

Leontyne then went on to play other exciting and important roles. In 1966, she played Cleopatra in the opera *Antony and Cleopatra*, based on the play written by William Shakespeare. It was the first show the Met held at its new location. The show did not get the best reviews. But Leontyne had sung beautifully.

Leontyne in her costume as Cleopatra.

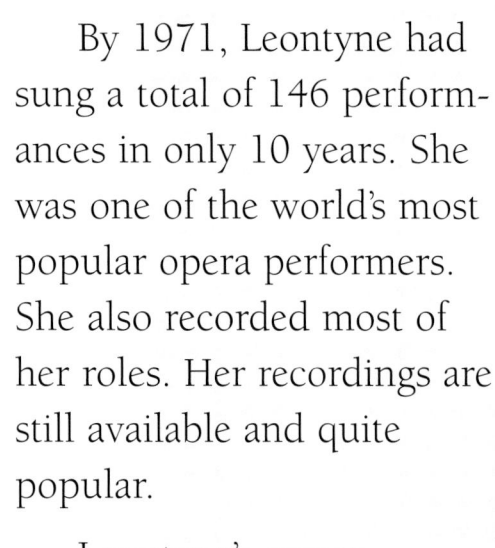

Leontyne became one of the most popular opera singers in the world.

By 1971, Leontyne had sung a total of 146 performances in only 10 years. She was one of the world's most popular opera performers. She also recorded most of her roles. Her recordings are still available and quite popular.

Leontyne's career changed a lot in the 1970s. She had more time between her performances. She started to devote herself to concerts and recitals. And she rested before and after all performances.

In 1977, Leontyne Price turned 50 years old. Her voice was still beautiful. But she wanted to leave the opera while her voice was still good. She did not want to stay too long.

For her final Metropolitan Opera performance, Leontyne decided to appear in the role of *Aïda*. She gave her final performance in 1985. It was broadcast live on the Public Broadcasting Service (PBS).

From that point on, Leontyne devoted her time to giving occasional recitals, teaching young opera singers, and tending her garden.

Leontyne remained active in music after her career ended. In 1990, she wrote and published a book. It was called *Aïda: A Picture Book for All Ages, As Told by Leontyne Price.*

In January 1992, Leontyne gave two recitals in Naples, Florida. Naples has a beautiful concert hall and a large symphony orchestra.

Leontyne chats with her idol, singer Marian Anderson, at a benefit concert.

Leontyne was able to relax and enjoy singing without the high pressure of a staged performance.

Teaching also became very important to her. She taught classes to voice students. She had become a mother figure to many black singers. Many young people visited Leontyne at her home in New York City. She would offer them advice on their careers.

Leontyne received a lifetime achievement award at the 1989 Grammy Awards.

Leontyne performs in Mozart's opera *Don Giovanni*.

    Today, Leontyne Price is known as one of the greatest opera singers of the twentieth century. She achieved success despite racism and segregation. There were black opera singers before her, but very few of them shone as brightly as Leontyne Price.

Glossary

Amateur Not professional.

Debut First appearance.

Discrimination To expose differences and treat people according to those differences.

Role model A person whom others want to imitate or look up to.

Segregation Separation.

Talent A special or creative artistic ability.

For More Information

Websites

Leontyne Price
www.shs.starkville.k12.ms.us/mswm/MSWritersAndMusicians/musicians/Price.htm

A student put together this comprehensive website that includes a biography, discography, and photographs, as well as an audio clip.

African American History: Leontyne Price
www.triadntr.net/~rdavis/price.htm

A brief biography and "flash facts" about Price.

Books

McNair, Joseph D. *Leontyne Price (Journey to Freedom)*. Chanhassen, MN: Child's World Inc., 2000.

Price, Leontyne. *Aïda*. Orlando: Harcourt, 1997.

Index

Aïda, 21, 26, 28
Antony and Cleopatra, 25

Central State University, 11-13
Chisolms, the 7-8, 13, 23
Curtain ceremony, 25

Divorce, 22-23

Falstaff, 16-17

Greer, Everlina, 7-8

Juilliard School, 13, 15

Kimball, Florence, 15

Laurel, Mississippi, 4, 7
Lincoln Center, 24
Lumber industry, 7

Metropolitan Opera, 14, 21, 23-24, 27

Naples, Florida, 28

Oak Park Vocational High School, 8

Piano lessons, 5
Porgy and Bess, 16-18
Price, George, 4, 11
  James Anthony, 4
  Katherine Baker, 4

Scholarship, 11
Segregated south, 7

Teaching voice, 29
Television roles, 21
Tosca, 20

Warfield, William, 17, 22-23

92 PRI
McCluer South-Berkeley Senior High School
2935387
Leontyne Price : singing star